Why Trees Stay Outside

By Terry Tierney

For information contact:
Unsolicited Press
Portland, Oregon
www.unsolicitedpress.com
orders@unsolicitedpress.com
619-354-8005

Cover Design: Kathryn Gerhardt
Editor: S.R. Stewart

ISBN: 978-1-963115-08-6

DEDICATION

So many people have supported and encouraged me during my journey that I risk leaving someone out, so please forgive any omissions.

My list always starts with Michaelyn Burnette, followed by my graduate school chums, including Jeffrey Portnoy, Kristina Straub, William Ellenburg, Rand and Beth Brandes, and our poet laureate Nathalie Anderson; lifelong friends Allan and Barbara Urbanic, Dave Fogarty, and Felicity Bensch; my poetry support system including Bruce Isaacson and Poetry Promise, Jan Steckel, Keith Gaboury, the California Writer's Club, and the San Francisco Writer's Grotto; the tireless and helpful editors and team at Unsolicited Press; my tolerant and loving family including Joan Northup, Janet Lafayette, Patricia Dahlman, and particularly John Tierney who gifted me the title poem; and my eager hiking buddy, Pearl, who often hears my words first.

ACKNOWLEDGEMENTS

The Author expresses his deepest gratitude to the literary journals and anthologies where these poems first appeared.

"Ashes on Water" *Trouvaille*
"Birth Cave" *Metaworker*
"Cleaning Out the Shed" *Sheila Na Gig*
"Ghost Machine" *Metaworker*
"His Sweatshirt" *Scapegoat Review*
"Hunter and Prey" *Commuter Lit*
"I Can't Get My Hands Clean" *Remington Review*
"It Starts with Hemingway" *Remington Review*
"The James Webb Telescope Detects a Heartbeat" *Bellevue Literary Review*
"Kissing My Grandmother at Her Funeral" *Words and Whispers*
"Lint" *Reed Magazine*
"Man in Glass" *Rogue Agent*
"1918 Reunion at Mountain View Cemetery" *The Town, An Anthology of Oakland Poets*
"Peeling the Handle" *Front Porch Review*
"Redwoods Whisper" *The Town, An Anthology of Oakland Poets*
"River Walk" *Green Light Literary Journal*
"Robot Writes a Love Poem" *Typishly*
"Rumor of Love" *The Blood Pudding*
"Spark" *Amethyst Review*
"Vacant Lot" *The Town, An Anthology of Oakland Poets*
"Waiting Out the Storm" *Poppy Road Review*
"Why Trees Stay Outside" *Rust & Moth*

POEMS

1—Faces in the Waiting Room

Front Line	15
Lint	17
Why Trees Stay Outside	19
Starlings at Sunset	21
Ghost Machine	22
Factory of Silent Women	24
I Can't Get My Hands Clean	25
Fallen	26
Next Wave	27
Kissing My Grandmother at Her Funeral	28
It Starts with Hemingway	30
His Sweatshirt	31
Einstein's Hair in Quarantine	33
Spark	35
My Genes Look Good on You	37
What Your Mother Saved	39
1918 Reunion at Mountain View Cemetery	41

2—Ashes on Water

Map and Compass	45

The Last Scarecrow 47

Planning My Garden 49

Redwoods Whisper 50

Woodpecker 52

Psychotherapy After Dinner 54

Questioning the Oranges 56

Photograph Smile 58

Morning Prayer 60

The Secret of Eternal Life 61

Birth Cave 62

Wake-Up Kiss 64

Ashes on Water 66

No Time Left 68

A Father's Prayer 70

Chainsaw Concerto 71

Painting a Still-life at Summer Solstice 73

3—Heartbeat

The James Webb Telescope Detects a Heartbeat 77

Car Trouble 78

Waiting Out the Storm 80

Black Ice 81

When God Collects the Rent 83

Cleaning Out the Shed 84

Running Away from Home   85

Coltrane Freeze   86

Papier-mâché of Promises   87

The Wait   89

Campfire   90

Owl on the Roof   91

River Walk   93

Wind Power   94

Man in Glass   95

New Year Morning 2021   96

Weatherman   97

4—Inheritance

Things You Learn in Bootcamp   101

Hunter and Prey   103

Inheritance   105

Vacant Lot   106

Bureaucracy on the Beach   107

Maybe the Sun   109

Peeling the Handle   110

Footsteps   112

Rose Boy   113

Letter from Home   115

I Died to Write This Poem   116

Fear of Spring   118

Rumor of Love   119

Again the Supermoon   120

Correction   121

Robot Writes a Love Poem   122

Interview for a Job as Poet   123

Why Trees Stay Outside

1—FACES IN THE WAITING ROOM

FRONT LINE

In the waiting room at the hospital
the narthex where we enter the world and leave

where a man in loose khakis
pushes a vacuum too fast
to pick up name tags, crumbs, tissues,
gravel from the parking lot

while outside through unshaded windows
a dog with careless stripes
its tail raised in a question mark
chases a gray squirrel behind the ambulance

why does the dog bother
guarding us from ourselves
our arms clutched on suffering benches
eyes praying for miracles of birth and death

the television blaring with gray news
battlefield in winter
a highway bends too close to the sky
scrapes bombs from clouds

leaves a billow of smoke
where our faces reflect on the display
like ridges of bones beneath torn sheets

while an old man at the chess board
fingers mismatched pieces, checks his pulse
wonders when they will call his number

why there are no windows to the back driveway
where the hearses wait, engines idling

behind the crackling screen
and the soft static of faces fading

LINT

Once you believed in God,
but each year he grew smaller, shrinking
like that cotton shirt you never wear,
the one with crossed oars, faded canoe,
Northwoods Bible Camp where you almost drowned.

The last time you saw him he was curled up
in the back row of your sock drawer,
hardly larger than the cotton ball
you saved from a bottle of Vitamin C.

By now he must be reduced to lint.
You recall the sermon in the camp clearing,
how faith is like lint: modest, unobtrusive,
but sticky in a tactile, textile way.
Bits of lint cling together, form a mass
like the congregation on your dryer filter
until it might fill a fluffy bear, flannel shirt,
stuffing for your wayward soul, a person, a saint.
The pastor shows her ball of lint with pride
but it could infer one god or many. Depends on faith
and faith depends on lint.

Alone in the deep lake you try to find him,
his tufty beard, grandfather on cresting wave,
though heaven must be farther away,

beyond reach, like the distant boat trailing
a weave of linty rope. Rescue or revelation?
Sinking boy never asks.

WHY TREES STAY OUTSIDE

Why do trees stay outside?
my son asks in the rearview mirror,
his car seat centered behind me.
He worries about the soaking rain,
the trees getting wet.

I could tell him the old fable:
the night the redwoods came to dinner
and grew too tall to leave.
Or I could tell him the truth,

how the trees are inside now.
We live in their house,
their roots clasped in rings around us
like praying hands. They watch,

wondering why we neglect
the pain of mowed grass,
the desperation of doe and fawn
sprinting for shelter, the cold stars
peering through boughs of live oak,
the promise of blooming moss.

I might echo his teachers,
say we are one with nature,
the trees and rocks love us.

They want to be left outside,
the easy answer he expects.

We climb a ridge as the rain clears,
sifting soot from the air.
Across the bay the Farallon Islands
punch through the fog like knuckles.

STARLINGS AT SUNSET

Starling songs expand and bend:
their yearning and vibrant murmurs
pour into silence of parked cars,
grounded jets, muffled whispers
behind face masks and plastic shields.
You trace their chorus in the distance,
discrete notes too high for human ears,
and follow their Rorschach cloud
twisting above wires like flowing ink
projecting images on your skin:
silhouettes of discarded lovers,
tattoos you never purchased,
all those places you lived melting
puddles in the smoke of memory.
Kneading air, the flock folds back,
a film blending past and future,
flaunting their immunity to time,
your fears, like the prayers you scrawl
on vellum and pin to the temple door
until the freshening wind lifts the edges
and swirls your hymn into wings.

GHOST MACHINE

My mother says the camera steals souls—
flash bulb explodes and collapses,
sucking spirits through shutters and lens,
ghostly fog on silver nitrate—

Edison's last invention,
a way to reverse the process,
ghost machine to call the dead
fails because they already answered,
hanging on damp Smithsonian walls.

You see them in prints from Antietam,
stoic generals, and twisted dead
souls raining down on fences and pasture,
wagon wheels stuck in spirit mud,

Matthew Brady's pine boxes
stuffed with ghosted plates,
Red Cloud his proud nose,
the prairie woman's scarred face
she says she remembers.

Album of souls on her coffee table,
family photos I scan to cloud,
even those from her funeral
that day I left my umbrella home

and learned that some escape,

her spirit seeping through my coat,
making sure I'll never forget.

FACTORY OF SILENT WOMEN

Watching them, my tiny ears fill
with buzzing cotton, clinking bells,
windless swooshes, gushing belts,
fearful slams of punch presses
spitting out clangs and scrap.

My nose presses against the glass,
my condensation of questions,
watching them assemble more machines,
the smell of oil and sparks,
floor crunchy with slivers and curls.

They wear their hair short,
lopped at the ears or tied in bandanas,
cheeks smudged with grit and soot,
arms thick with pits and scratches,
bracelets chained to switches.

First one and then another
the line of women finds my face,
the look of my mother sending me off to school,
silent goodbyes in the crushing noise
until they all yell at once.

I CAN'T GET MY HANDS CLEAN

She's sure to notice
even after all this time.

She knows every mote of dust,
syllables left by our conversations,
the words I allowed to escape,
the black line in the scar on my thumb.

If only flesh would seal that chasm
and fill the shallow crosses of fingerprints,
greasy scratches, and gray-pink shadows,
embedded grit that engines shed like spores
as if they will sprout new cams and pistons.

She used to worry about my hands
not because of their coarse edges
snagging the cotton of her blouse,
but the way she could read a man's grasp,
the garages where he worked.

The nights she peeled back my skin
and found another layer of stained callus
no matter how deep I scrubbed.

FALLEN

One jagged maple leaf
suspended like skin on wet clay,
sharp red points around a yellow bow,
the center green, a cupped palm.
I treat it like the gift it is
though it doesn't remember
the chaos of spring, the waning mist,
summer so hot the asphalt steamed,
the forced retirement of autumn.
Then silence like duct tape
denying the blood I still feel,
hands that reach for the leaf,
moss and bark that cover my ribs,
the tangle of branches lifting my heart.
In this dark chasm of a dried stream
there's moisture if I dig deep enough,
the stem of nameless hope
sifting the dust for pollen.

NEXT WAVE

She listens to surf until it stops,
rollers held in crest, tide pool still,
anemone petals fixed like spikes.

Falling to beach, her face drains,
pain fading with consciousness.

Bystanders find no pulse,
punch her chest two inches deep,
cracking ribs,
one hundred strikes per minute,
keep her brain alive,
the briny sounds and swells.

Medics arrive,
placing paddles upper left, lower right,
semaphore code for Reset,
shock and bouncing trunk.
Again, again.

Foam at wave's peak
extends like a brush stroke,
falls and swirls, feeding pools,
etching sand with broken shells,
flowing back to sea.

KISSING MY GRANDMOTHER AT HER FUNERAL

Makeup on her cheeks pink like a doll,
scent of perfume tinged with chemicals,
her grim smile as if she knows the secret,
no hug from her folded arms, no return kiss,
no plate of cookies to reward my visit.
Powder coats my lips like floured dough.
I follow the family line, my silent carnation,
the altar piled with bouquets and photos
like butterflies pinned to cardboard,
her casket much too heavy for her, too large,
her body shrunken, light enough to float.
Her soul might have risen already, curling
with smoke from the men hovering nearby,
their mingled whispers, their memories,
recalling her sly sense of humor, a few jokes
muffled by the organ procession on tape.
Some say she will wait in damp clay
until that moment when all emerge at once,
each breaking through their wood chrysalis.
How will I find her among the crowd,
her tiny figure, her outsized dress?
Her cosmetic face, cheeks much too firm,
cold as batter from her icebox?
My eyes dim with tears, unmanly,

hoping no one else is watching.
Will I even be there? Yes, of course,
she says in her private voice.
Now don't be silly.

IT STARTS WITH HEMINGWAY

Hunched over black typewriter,
musing light, sun-washed curtains,
cigarette targeting keys,
another burning in glass ashtray.

Sleeveless, fly-sticking sweat,
he slams the carriage return:
rifle bolt spitting empty shells,
platen injecting a new line.
Polydactyl cat on windowsill.

Same cat perches in my chair
matted fur from trekking north.
Key West to Miami by boat,
padding through snaky swamps,
canvas vest stuffed with flasks--
sultry whisky and cognac promise,
carton of Camels in backpack.

Typing fast with six toes,
no thumb for space bar,
endless paragraph unrolling
toward asphalt horizon,
word to word, strangers no more.
Kerouac asleep in the back.
My turn to drive.

HIS SWEATSHIRT

You ask me what he likes to eat
but I only remember his sweatshirt
gray like a sun-blanched tent,
more thread than weave at the edges.

He never cared about seams,
all flaps open to the wind
even in the broken glass of winter
the night he brought me a potted jade
its lower leaf puckered and brown
like an old man's face.

He said you gave him the plant
and he wanted me to keep it
as if my apartment were a museum
he might visit on Sundays
when the admission was free.

But I never asked him for anything
not even the shaker of salt
when we ate the ears of corn I boiled.

He preferred them roasted on the grill
but it was my beer, my kitchen
where we grew old telling stories about you,
how he used to be your lover
or maybe he invented that.

I wish I could say he ate well
but he left random kernels on the cob
like broken teeth, a music roll
he might play back if I had a piano,
notes bouncing ragtime but sad,
the way he could reach into your soul.

You told me that once,
the morning we awoke in Montana
when I thought you were talking about me.

EINSTEIN'S HAIR IN QUARANTINE

My head grows Einstein's hair
but I lost his relativity.

I search in old man pockets,
lint absorbing inky sweat,

timeless creases of laundry.
Paper flakes and chalky dust

clump in blistered nose,
seeding the wisps of wiry clouds.

My clothes hang like galaxies,
translucent, strands of gravity,

equations erased and rewritten
like a loom weaving warps of yarn

until the weft ends, returns.
Errant fibers sprout from dark moles,

bend with light, vectors of memory
cradled in Einstein's nest.

The barber waits with warm towels.
His eyes offer no advice, no solution,

but in his foxed mirror a new reality,
a theory I must relearn.

SPARK

*In Bleak House, by Charles Dickens, a
character's death is attributed to spontaneous
combustion.*

You say he deserved it,
rag collector, slumlord
mining misery from broken tenants,
any coin for a flask of gin,
his bloated body like an artillery shell
with fumes straining its rusted case.

Until the spark ignites and wicks
inside his windpipe, chases
saturated blood through arteries,
devouring his flesh in seconds.
Cloud of oily smoke hangs over
his bed, ash on last night's dinner,
scraps of bread not even a dog will eat.

No sign of match strike or boot scuff,
no storm clouds releasing their charges
across the sky of his room. The spark
arose inside him, as if he balanced
his internal ledger, always a gap,
flint spleen scratching rib, or vertebrae
gnashing against forgiveness,
then the flash like a wink of usury.

You say his bedding survived,
his legs still planted in leather soles,
his hands extended toward the table,
the loose bundle of bills, glass of spirit,
as if he thirsted for one last swallow,
one more squeeze for his still heart
now melted into the charred trunk
of his body, compressed like coal.

Easy to fault the gin, the fermented soul,
but what if you misread his gesture,
what if he reached for his papers
to rend their threads like a widow's clothes,
a surprise cancellation, an epiphany.

MY GENES LOOK GOOD ON YOU

DNA mutates in close contact,
the way you and I mix our fluids, our blood.

If someone clipped our genes now
what a monster they could build.

My gin-pocked nose,
your smooth face
now sprouting unruly whiskers,
hair falling from your head in clumps,
my rotting roof over your aspirations
and yes, my lunchbox dreams.

You would think your hands too large,
I my legs too short
and what is that between them?

What should we call ourselves
as we lumber through space,
two planets mashed together
by cynical biology

recalling those earthquake nights
when the safe distance of orbit
was the wiser path

but we both knew it was not enough,
no way to stop our dangerous gravity,
fill the empty yearning of our cells.

WHAT YOUR MOTHER SAVED

No one's in the photograph,
no one you know. But your mother kept it.
She might have taken the snapshot,
tilting the aim of her red box camera,
asking the two women to stand near blooming lilacs
where sunlight glints through branches of elm,
ignites their squinting eyes and dry smiles,
arms draped over shoulders and fingers stretched
as if they clicked the shutters themselves.
But there's no sun you can see
outside the frame, nor the secrets they hide
behind their wispy hair and floral dresses
tugged by light wind, tiny hands of breath
you cannot smell. No one else is watching,
no one you know, no one to hear what they said
before the camera winked and after,
how they planned their holiday
that summer after Pearl Harbor, begging off work,
their frayed hems restitched, how they waited
for the Rexall Drugstore to develop the film,
dark negatives with ghostly gray figures
and the prints they sent to their boyfriends overseas
like the photo you hold, smudged by fingertips,
your mother's. You imagine these events,
producing a documentary in your mind,
an afternoon she remembered but why,
something lost or treasured, someone

among all the unseen moments, faces,
words forgotten as if unspoken. No one to hear.
Only you under the yellow reading lamp
casting a focus they cannot see.

1918 REUNION AT MOUNTAIN VIEW CEMETERY

We rise and gather on Armistice Day
for the irony, Werner's idea,
after surviving Pershing's offensive
disaster with only a leg wound,
then slain by Spanish Flu
in the Oakland auditorium.

Nearby, Florence the lively one
who refused a mask, too KKK.
She's 1919 but one of us,
her children forever infants
yearning to play in the grass.

From the unmarked slope
Irish laborers who rolled us here
remark the view that winter,
silent city, no ships moving,
chapel flag blowing half-mast.

Like them I crave the air on the ridge
after my hours of straining breath,
chest rising full but empty.
Ocean breeze like a sweet cigar
after the night of fading stories.

My wife awaits as ever,
complaining about the hour,
smoke she cannot smell,
her dry cough. I feel so helpless,
wishing I had another blanket
to wrap her shivering pain,
if only I could reach her.

2—ASHES ON WATER

MAP AND COMPASS

They blew up the town to build a freeway,
flooded another to enclose a reservoir--
you see the steeple rise in drought years
like the black speck on your X-ray, wishing
you only swallowed something by mistake.

Every operation is a choice,
every choice an incomplete secret,
the artifacts no one remembers
buried beneath years of blood and rubble,
the cage of your skeleton, your mind
reaching out for any chance of escape.

Whoever drew the old map is dead now,
their GPS signals are all we have left
if that's the myth you want to believe,
satellite souls in orbit, cold and accurate,
directions ever precise.

They have no need for taste and touch,
for how a fetus finds its way to life,
how deer smell an arriving storm,
birds know the layers of air, phases
of moon and sun, the seasons.

We describe geography like a living body:
arms of land, breath of wind, the tide

reaching over sand like a lover awakening,
the way I trace the nerves along your spine,
my need to cover your body with my own,
protect you from the threat of change.

THE LAST SCARECROW

Black and yellow flannel shirt
and polished cotton pants he hated
hold the flex of his shoulders, his knees,
the smell of his work. He built me from scrap
though he always joked that I created him.

The day his corkscrew machine
pried open the soil, corn kernels
becoming a cache for crows and jays,
robins too polite to dig deeply.
Now sparrows pick lice from my seams.

The bugs should know I have no blood,
only this reservoir of regret wishing
he had given me a name, flipped our identities,
made me Willet, and he the scarecrow
threatening birds with bare sticks,
watching the wiry dog chase the wind.

While I fall in love, learn to play chess,
bury my wife, plant azaleas behind her painted rock.
Molly had the skin of summer, warm to the touch
he said, and I still taste her breath
as frost chases leaves down the hillside,
raises spikes on its bald crest.

That morning he drove away
lying in the back of a tinted SUV,
hardly a ripple in my singular shadow,
the daily circle it draws on fallow and chaff
like crows searching for seed,
always searching.

PLANNING MY GARDEN

Call of wind raking chords
over winter's stems, songbirds
flying octaves higher, drone
of hatching insects.

My fingers twitch, imagining dirt,
clawing down a staircase of roots,
each grip as slow as reading,
like redwoods probing a gully
strewn with boulders and abandoned cars,
baking tins exploded with rust,
rounded corners of appliances.

There an underground kitchen
hangs with carrots and garlic,
damp flowerpots on the sill.
A gopher chants recipes
from her pulpit of sifted loam.

I bend my dry husk of scalp
bulging with seeds attached by filament
until they pop out the cracked hull
ready to sprout.

REDWOODS WHISPER

Fog thick with souls of birds,
the stale scent of smoke,
last night's wildfire, blood red sunset
like peering through a thick Merlot.

We drink without joy
embraced by roots of redwoods,
the ones we managed to preserve.

What do the redwoods see in us?
They wish they could walk away.
They hear the beehive in our skulls
wings pulling in every direction,

they foresee our shredding bark
crumbled and empty
the structures we built from native rock,
our wood-framed rooms,
the scrape of steel edges

until our machines die
and the only tools are held by crows,
road cuts left for paw and cloved hoof.

They fear we will be replanted,
our burls sprouting new ambitions.

They know how hard we try to save them.
There is only one way to save them.

WOODPECKER

Loud knocks at daybreak
when I should be dreaming,
the echo inside my brain
like the creep of another migraine
filling the hollow of rotting wood.

I know what the rhythm means.
Soft studs and peeling paint
weathered by heat and too little rain,
the dry rot of good intentions,
but this summer I will make repairs
unless my hammer hangs too heavy
like last year, that morning he left.

Outside my window the woodpecker
stares back with one hollow eye,
white crown with a splash of red,
gray and black streaks like bark
as if that camouflage would fool me.

Splayed talons press against shingles,
hold the wall steady,
balanced over the steep hill
inaccessible but to flying things
as if the house were built top down,
a cable descending by crane
from clouds of memory.

There are things I want to say:
how I finally breathed when he was gone,
how coming back as bird or angel
will not change anything,
how I wish he would have stayed,
how my arms ache from driving alone,
how my fists clench every time I hear him,
my eyes sealed with salt.

When the hole is large enough
I know the woodpecker will bury
another acorn, a scrap of soul,
the way he watches me
even after he flies away.

PSYCHOTHERAPY AFTER DINNER

When she unzips her sweater,
her lungs spill to the floor,
still humming the soundtrack
of our dinner conversation,
our sticky choice of dessert,
how we tasted the pollen in honey,
the way she knitted the carnation
on her pocket, a finer yarn
tacking the blossom like the veins
connecting her stomach as it slides
out between the flaps of her jeans.
Then the long trails of intestines,
silvery serpents smelling of souls,
the salmon and wild rice, the wine.
I worry about her gentle heart,
whether it can take the pressure,
the jarring fall to hardwood,
but it purrs between her womb
and her fertile lobes of brain.
Her long legs and slender arms
detach and curl around her organs,
and her ribs pull away like butterflies
until only her spine stands wavering,
an empty hanger bent straight
with nothing left to stretch,
collapsing beside her shoes.
From her warm pile of blood and flesh

I feel her fingertips emerge, crawling
up my ankles, past my waist
to my own peeling hand,
helping me unbutton my shirt.

QUESTIONING THE ORANGES

We conjugate irregular verbs,
German trills that make me smile,
our bellies full from lunch of hamburger casserole,
when the loudspeaker belches like an air raid:
President Kennedy shot and killed.
Buzz-click, silence.

Leaning on her crutches, our German teacher,
forearms pressing leather straps
unclenched for chalk and pointers,
says he would have wanted us to continue,
her elusive perfect tense trying to sooth.

How did she feel
when she watched the brothers
tossing footballs in black and white?
When the Sachs vaccine arrived
too late for her?

My mother says orange peels cause polio
though Vitamin C prevents it,
one of those anomalies
like how a young woman with perfect English
teaches German in Minneapolis.

Did she flee the war
or one of those ethnic towns like New Ulm
thriving behind a wall of language
with long German nouns trailing like ivy,
irregular verbs on every tongue?

Do they crave the danger of oranges there,
stripping away white flakes of peel
and clinging strands
until just the inner skin and pulp
burst with sticky sweet juice?

Some still say oranges are cause and cure,
Kennedy is not really dead,
and my German teacher is a genius—
that much is true. How else to explain
the awe of fourteen-year-olds,
her quick response to every mistake,
every question.

Except the ones we are afraid to ask:
What really happened during the war?
What did the killer see in his scope?
What will happen to us now?
And what about the seeds--
is it safe to eat the seeds?

PHOTOGRAPH SMILE

My young son learned to smile on cue,
lips curling tight around jaw,
cheeks puffed by new muscle,
eyes gleaming with impatience.

In the stack of prints we saved
he smiles the same year by year
as teeth pierce his gums,
fall and rise again larger.

I watch his blue eyes turn wary,
headlights scanning beyond the camera
as if he's grown tired of life already,
the snap of portrait burning
deeper than lasers.

Now we share the wheel,
with Beatles blaring from the deck
as we cross the high plains,
avoid glances and small talk,
how I wanted to protect him,
how he hides his pain,
his judgment, too much like me.
Until the riffs of "Here Comes the Sun"
and the sky splits with rain.

Blinded by water, we creep ahead,
caught in a car bubble of time,
an unpracticed smile, our eyes joining
in a slash of lightening.

MORNING PRAYER

I climb an extinct volcano tipped on its side,
cliff shore of a former sea, third year of drought.
Each morning my neighbor searches for water,
avoids my eyes, my mumbled hello, crosses
to the far side of the trail. My shoes fill with sand.
Squirrels scold me for stepping on fallen plums.

In Kamakura, my friend pulled me aside
not to disturb a priest climbing the stairs,
the fog of the early morning Shinto shrine,
his wooden sandals clapping on worn granite,
the rhythm of his silent prayer as he raised his knees
to gain each step, his jōe washed in rain.

The temple path leads from nearby ocean,
layers of plum blossoms under our feet.
I wonder if he pitied me, read my pain,
if he saw me at all, if the squirrels
paused when he passed, or I forgot to listen,
straining to see the altar's hissing flame.

Here I never dare to light a fire.
I have no incense, no patience for gods,
their indifference, their coded messages,
their silence. But I remember the squirrels,
the strides I take before each dawn, sand
griding the moist web between my toes.

THE SECRET OF ETERNAL LIFE

You drop your empties in a gray bin
if they are stamped with one or two.
Other numbers join unsorted trash.

But beyond the wire gate of the landfill
all numbers are reunited, waiting
for the ultimate sorter to recycle all.
We trust the myth of our technology.

Mystics talk of regeneration,
how our bodies dissolve into plants
or higher lives, souls rising to the top.

They float among that mass in the Pacific
with miles of Styrofoam, your old cooler,
wheels from your daughter's first bike,
one-use bags, the fossil oil that formed them:

how we achieve immortality,
rapture spinning on ocean currents,
our creations timeless, names
engraved on plastic Visa cards.

BIRTH CAVE

Shaman paints the wolf
and full moon blister red
above a sinuous line of orange scales,
serpent tail pointing to the past,
head spitting a speckled frog
half digested, white eyes lifeless.

One more sweep of horsetail brush
and they wink awake--one more
chance to escape--legless
mind ascends in sparks.

Wolf sniffs the new stars,
remembers all wolves
as a child knows its mother,
curling mouth to tail,
warm den moist and rich
denying the dark worm of night.

Outside branches claw
thin veins in snow crusts,
frozen rivulets of glacier blood,
moonlight eclipsed by earth's heart
beating in its rib-cave of wind.

Brush extends, tail
soft and slick with paint,

tongue licking the edge
of my mouth. Yellow eyes
stare at the burning hole,
my lungs explode.

WAKE-UP KISS

Eyelids sticky with salt,
tight in their rolls, broken shades
filtering light through filmy windows,

the shopping cart on the sidewalk,
the laurel where every dog pisses,
the pile of blankets I left outside
for a reason I can't remember.

That leaky conversation
when I embarrassed myself,
revealed how lonely I was,
the all-night diner with bottomless coffee,
wishing I had a tree to pee on,

knowing she had money,
though I would never ask her for any
nor bring her to my narrow space
lined with tarps and spiderwebs.

But there we were,
my drunken apologies hardly mattered,
the rumble of jets careening above us,
plaster dust on worn sheets,
the damp chill,

knowing I left my ribs open too long
the way I shook awake
before sunrise, coughing alone
on the waxy stain of lipstick.

ASHES ON WATER

Watching his color drain,
I recall the brown river,
rusty film of steel mills and cracked oil
coating water, caking windows,
sticking to soles of our shoes.
Acres of perch float belly up.

One day the river catches fire.
Dirty rose sunset over city,
wild flames climb the hills,
blowing down in orange rings,
clogging streams with dead trees,
lungs coughing acid smoke,
the dust of lives.

Pink river of phlegm
carving new channels down his chin.
Drying his lips with cotton balls,
the wet metallic scent,
steel roses burning.

That day roofing my house,
his hand gripping hammer,
oily smell of nails, tar, and sweat,
cigarettes glowing after dusk,
thirsting for a better ending.

Under a blood orange sun,
Cane Creek rolls with pink flecks,
yellow pine dust clogs the air.
They spill his ashes above the falls,
rushing cold and clear.

NO TIME LEFT

My parents never told me
the clock was beyond repair,
knocked from the dresser doily,
busted open like a cantaloupe
with tiny screws and levers
hanging on loose springs
or lying free, some lost.

My small fingers hover for hours
retrying the threads, twisting the band,
bending the hands straight,
even their V-shaped arrows,
patient to hear a tick.

How old before I put it away,
the puzzle of brass and steel,
always finding more notches,
more holes to fill.
Why did I keep it?

Now my friend stands
at office door asking advice:
should he sign a lease,
get married in March,

how many days do we have?
His hands hang open
but I have nothing to give him.
We both know the company is failing.

Even if I aligned the cams and gears,
found something to reconnect.
Even if I had all the pieces.

A FATHER'S PRAYER

Why do I pray for you
if I don't believe in prayer
and you are too old to hear
words from any god or me?
I would surrender another rib
if it made a difference,
if the bowed weight it held
rang in minor thirds, a bridge
strung between verses
we once sang together.

CHAINSAW CONCERTO

Fog leans against my window
though it never rains,
just the splintered groan of dying eucalyptus,
the scream of chainsaws
slicing through Vivaldi on my headphones.

Through the haze a man tied to the trunk
leans like a gargoyle, head and arms extended,
sawdust spilling from fresh cuts,
shouts in Spanish I cannot understand
though I ordered the work,
displaced the squirrels and jays.

No need to explain to them
the oily tinder of bark and branches,
ominous scent of cough drops,
bloody glow of smoke at sunset,
how the eucalyptus don't belong here,

how I left my shuttered hometown for work,
its river thick with silt and carp,
walls streaked with moss, the mildewed towels,
the humid summer I read *The Alexandria Quartet,*
another expatriate migrating west
like wild turkeys from the Rio Grande,
like most things here
even the violin concerto.

Fog cups the sound like taunts of rain
while roots of a native oak grip the eroded hillside
lifting a gnarled limb
where a turkey spends the night.

PAINTING A STILL-LIFE AT SUMMER SOLSTICE

Glass jar reflects the heat.
Refracted stems of asters, sprig of lilac
pierces the water's skin,

the convex image of something deeper
your face smaller than you expect.

Oranges and green apple
placed to seem random, white towel
to catch the shadow cast by perfect light
sticky with sap.

Brush strokes
streaked with pollen
trap the buzz of insects,
the blue echo of birds stroking wind,
the ozone scent of afternoon rain.

And before your work is finished
stars hover like peering eyes.

You strain to stretch the gloaming moment,
hold back the night.

3—HEARTBEAT

THE JAMES WEBB TELESCOPE DETECTS A HEARTBEAT

They say the pulses come from a distant galaxy,
an infant cluster in the first moment of birth.

But I wonder if the heartbeat is yours
there in your nebula of blood and gas
mindlessly chewing the corners of your blanket
with toothless gums,
your eyes still shut to screaming light,

the weave of distance and time
where you will always be our first child,
the edge of our farthest vision.

We squint in every spectrum
just to see you the way you are
though we know it's the way you were
what you might have been,

larger than we can imagine
and farther than any lost prayer,
your growth beyond our lifespan.

What do you see when you look our way:
are we even there or are we infants
like you?

CAR TROUBLE

When I meet my new neighbor
her blue Camaro sits on four flat tires
stabbed by a knife.

I help her change them,
my jack, her wrench, shuttling
each wheel to Mel's Repair Shop.

She left her husband in Memphis,
and I just moved to Atlanta to find work.
She keeps her distance.

One night I convince her
to visit the Little Five Points Pub
where beer runs cheaper than air.

We talk blue Camaros with spoke wheels
because all blondes like blue,
how I wish I owned her ride.

She laughs, shows darker roots,
the hometown name I can't pronounce
where everyone speeds away.

We end up making drunken love,
clutching each other like life preservers
bobbing for breath on her rented bed.

The next afternoon she calls me,
her voice deflated. She wrecked her car,
can I drive her to the doctor?

When I pick her up,
her face is bruised, her lip split.
From the accident, she claims.

Her eyes blink wide and sharp,
a signal I read too late,
pickup in the rearview mirror.

WAITING OUT THE STORM

Lightning flares my windows,
carves the edge of darkness
with storm clouds of agony,
low groan of rock on rock.

Broken stumps line the road,
stripped of bark, roots clutching dirt
like corpses gripping dry sheets,
the death rattle of fallen branches.

Sparkless cables lie uncoiled,
drained of voices, words lost to wind
dropping vowels like thankless gifts,
my lips gritty with sand.

Door swings on rusty hinges,
spilling a fingernail scratch of sky.
I have something more to say
before it slams shut.

BLACK ICE

That night I called you back
through storm door and wailing wind,
but you had to leave, ignoring
frost in all directions,
fog of our condensed passion,
words we should not have spoken,
frozen breath,

glaze on asphalt
your body senses too late,
unable to repel, no traction,
no reflection.

Friction brings warmth, you said,
like spinning tires on pavement.
I wish I could believe you now
as snow clouds descend.
I wish I could extend my arms
like a winch and pull you out.

Are you unwinding as you go
or are your tired fingers
clutching the wheel like mine?

I try to predict the wind, the next gust,
the way I overcompensate for happiness,
squeezing it for water, raising a thin mist

where I hide from our next argument
until it sparks despite the cold,
forms shadowy crystals.

WHEN GOD COLLECTS THE RENT

Limousine gleams under streetlamp,
angels leaning on fenders, airbrush perfect,
singing in harmony with their iPhones.
How old he looks, too old
for them, but I know better.

I hide behind my curtain, watch
his approach up cracked slate,
his weightless footsteps. He knows
where I stand, my thinning hair,
swollen joints, depleted cash.

He might have arrived by meteor,
a charging bull, golden warrior,
hunter who shoots first,
but he instills more fear like this,
cerebral and quiet.

When he rattles my door,
my breath dissolves in whispers,
words limping over threshold
practiced and hollow, pleading
give me a few more days.

CLEANING OUT THE SHED

Dented camping lantern,
ash sock fallen away, gray dust
lying somewhere between my shed
and the frame that brought me here:
old Ford rusting under blackberry,
straining to escape on shredded tires.

I recall that summer I pitched my tent,
stakes piercing sod at precise angles
between rocks and manure,
fooling the wind, so proud,
rain wicking from canvas roof,
tiny sphere of guttering light.

Now my feet slip on plywood floor
greased by winters of leaking fuel,
my shoulders scratch nail points
and planks replaced year by year
until the shadows deny their origin.

Mud oozes through rotting boards,
thick and rusty, a mildew smell
pulling me deeper, walls collapsing
as if I might never leave this place.
Toes grip to hold my balance
through cracked leather sole.

RUNNING AWAY FROM HOME

Every breath must be exhaled
the way his mother's open wound
transfers to him, never healing.

That night he refuses to sleep,
climbs out his bedroom window
to catch a cooling breeze,
the only air he wanted.

Alone in the backyard
his body breathes through mineral pores,
mass of untilled soil straining
to sprout between blackberry thorns
and spiral clips of hair.

We see the old man in the boy,
dried vine in eager tendril
as if change itself were the enemy,
knowing his mother will never forgive
how he left or his choice of guilt,
the freedom or the pain.

He hears the sun before he sees it,
light spilling like rain,
sutures always closing.

COLTRANE FREEZE

My mind weak and empty, hiding
with pulsing transistor under pillow,
the first muted solo through foamy flakes.
Notes drool down my chin.

Standing, I see fissures
where there should be sky:
Razor slash of sunset
veins trailing cold tresses,
threads drawn by hooked horn,
brassy smell of ice on skin.

Pressing my nose to window
pulled by minor scales of frost,
A Love Supreme etched in glass
like tiny fossil footprints.

Snowblind but for moon
waning crescent molting light
and edges of skin, calling in triplets
to cauterize my wounds.

PAPIER-MÂCHÉ OF PROMISES

I said I would quit this parking lot
but what to leave behind--
my excuse for staying another season.

If I were a hunter the geese would call,
instead they fly in pantomime angles
a direction I refuse to travel

like that night my car swerved
on collapsed shock absorbers,
the last time it started, my trunk
weighed down with snow chains
even in August when tires smolder,
my lunchbox clanging with every rut,
its decal scraped by shifting tools
despite the blankets and fast-food wrappers.

More sodden trash paves the asphalt,
pressed flat by countless wheels and feet,
the papier-mâché of promises, scraps
not firm enough to build a wall,
build a home.

St. Jude's Hospital and Guideposts
still send me mail like old friends

down on their luck, only temporary,
with recurring offers of redemption.
Why is it always about money?

THE WAIT

That place where we often met,
the driveway to the abandoned farm,

the smell of salty oil on your skin,
the faint perfume that clogs my breath,

your after-shadow in magenta and blue
as if a headlight flashed and faded.

I hear your cough in rasping branches,
sandal scuffs on loose gravel,

your smoky, sweet taste on my tongue.
I crave the oxygen you exhaled,

the saliva and sweat in every crease,
the soft impression of clay flesh,

our dew falling on cracks of mud.
That broken gate I never left.

CAMPFIRE

The last stick ignites,
a comet in a sky of embers
framed by our ring of rock planets.

Shadows on the edge of sight
cool and darken our straining faces
now ignited by the thin splash of light
short-lived, absorbed by blackness.

We lie naked, bodies in space
embraced by arms of gravity,
our collision shedding meteors:

words, promises sparking in air
until they fall back into cinders,
the fire's black hole.

Black the sum of all colors, the way
echoes of memory fade and merge,
their muted ringing in my ears,
the soundtrack of love enduring
like dark matter between stars.

OWL ON THE ROOF

Fog descends on gray water,
insects cluster on ropes of kelp,
gloaming light flashes like discarded glass
reflecting folds of mountains across the bay,
their shapes never changing.

My view is always the same,
slight backward tilt at my base,
my talons screwed to a board,
board nailed to the roof, fixed
horizon, clear days, storms,
sines and cosines of dolphin breaks,
messy whale spouts, sinister trawlers,
surfers challenging rip tide.

Seagulls land behind me like spies,
feet sticking to tar paper, taunt me with gawks,
think they are safe, that I am frozen,
that my weathered wings will never soar
above the light post where they nest,
never snap up the plumpest and sweetest,
carry it to the tufted crown of palm,
its trunk bent like twisted rope
hanging on a limb of sky.

But I can wait, I can control
my hunger. Molded in plastic,
I will live forever.

RIVER WALK

Melting spring reveals its treasures,
purity of snow fading to brown,
swampy scent of renewal
tinged with dog waste.

Rotting carp drags a wake
like the helm of a royal yacht
welcomed by flags of toilet paper.
Napkin blossoms line the shore.

Styrofoam peanuts sprout in green algae
with shiny nuggets of aluminum foil
and sapphire Doublemint wrappers.

Grocery bags unfold and swim
like jellyfish in the breeze.

Arrowhead bottle stranded ashore
behind a fence of dead reeds
and black shards, bobs in gray water,
reflects my distorted face.

WIND POWER

Wind seeps through fabric,
through your pores, blowing
outside to inside, never straight,
a flag unfurled, unpredictable,
starts in one direction and pivots,
dropping dust, leaves, insects, skin.

Spinning wind wraps your face,
drapes a shawl on every face,
circles the earth, eternal. One breath,
one stream of air fills every pocket,
fills sails, waters eyes, chills
through creases and seams.

Hunching over, bending skyward,
wind pushes your balance,
lifts your wings, your shirt,
your wisps of hair, the hood of your car
until you feel shortness of breath
and gasp like a tropical storm.

Unseen wind prowls your flesh,
canyons and valleys, raises heat,
shares your lungs with others,
presses your body shut,
draws it open.

MAN IN GLASS

Studies me, head tilting,
trying to center his gravity,
focus his lenses, frame twisted
to match his nose bridge
bent by an old punch.

Corners of lips turn downward,
one cheek dragging lower, minor stroke
or aging twist of bone and teeth,
gray stubble covering chin and jaw,
hiding his slack skin neck.

Above his beard line solitary hairs
sprout like saplings in a fallow field
among veins and wrinkles,
tributaries of sunken swamps
beneath his staring eyes.

He turns when I turn,
breaking away, image ejected
like a slide show from past summers.
No, that's not my face.

NEW YEAR MORNING 2021

Too early to get up.
My bladder alarm—ignore it.
If I roll over and stretch my legs
the dog will press her nose to my cheek,
demanding her morning walk.
So I lie still, pretending to sleep,
clutching warmth, hoping to return.
Pretending became a habit this past year,
hiding fears, apprehensions. Pandemic,
inequality, corrupt politicians, homeless--
when will I be next? Forget all that.
Empty my thoughts like a vacuum cleaner bag,
lint floating above my calm pillow.
Breathe slowly--a Tibetan monk--
think of nothing. Nothing. Nothing but
a strawberry. That bowl in the refrigerator,
are they still edible for breakfast?
The last box of cereal, Grape Nuts,
and the milk, no not the milk.
Tomorrow I will go shopping.
I will be a better man.
I will walk the dog for an hour,
vacuum her fur from the stained carpet.
I will eat Grape Nuts, rejoice in my stale bounty,
grateful to have something, anything.
I will devote my life to others
if only I can doze for ten more minutes.

WEATHERMAN

He knows it will rain when his knees swell,
bags of blood squeeze his grinding bones.

The dark days of no sun, his darker mood.
He measures the length of his limping strides,

projects their end, but today a short walk
like slathering grease on rusted rack and pinion.

He wonders if storms ever die or circle the earth forever,
drain weaker as they go, gather in tropical retreats,

sip umbrella drinks, collect crystals of shaved ice
until they blossom refreshed, bulging with carefree humidity.

He remembers that warm day his sun-dried bones flexed,
the swelling evaporated in steamy clouds,

skin baked and stretched like tanning leather,
free of pain, a comfort too much like death.

4—INHERITANCE

THINGS YOU LEARN IN BOOTCAMP

Machine gun fire sounds like downtown
only hotter, more persistent.

Tracer rounds burn holes in bone.

When the smoking lamp is lit you smoke
but look out for gooks sneaking up.

Even the women and children
pull the pin when you try to help them.

Your rifle is your wife.

Rockets and bombs can burst your ears.
Unsafe to sleep with ear plugs.

No one can flip a quarter on a bedsheet,
just an excuse to make you redo it.

Discipline will save your life.

Never trust a gook, even an ally.

Trust your rifle team, your squad.
We never leave anyone behind.

Watch your step, boobytraps, landmines.

They're all fanatics, all gooks,
little people out to kill us.

See the way they look at you.

HUNTER AND PREY

Alone, lying on my back
in a haystack of tundra,
arctic wilderness, no shade, no trees,
exposed under winking sun
and wet Aleutian wind.
I pull my parka tighter and watch
the black spec soaring over sawtooth ridge
circling once and heading toward me
too high for a gull, too large--
an eagle with wings broader
than my outstretched body.
A shiver enters my ankles
up along my jean hems
as if I were naked as a salmon
beneath its razor talons,
silver skin torn open on gray slate,
steaming pink flesh hanging
in strings from hooked beak.
The eagle spirals above me
ever lower and tighter,
spinning a vortex, lifting my mind
above my body. I see myself lying there,
dark in the sea of brown grass,
out of place to eyes that know
every crevice, every prey,
scanning my prone figure for a twist
of fin or gill, an open wound

from pounding water and sharp rock,
an easy catch or carrion, easier still.
The eagle swerves closer, opal eye
testing my parka's nylon skin,
the fevered flesh beneath,
and I force my breath to slow,
my tendons stretching to flip away,
reading no mercy, no fear,
just the predatory math of hunger and risk,
its own survival. With one more swoop
I wave my arms, but the eagle
tilts toward the shore.
I stare at congealed clouds
and the cold comfort of sudden rain.

INHERITANCE

We know she left by the silence,
breath held in cage of bone,
skin pulled tight in frigid air,
drying flesh, moisture receding,
joining the fluid that forms the earth.

Notepad on table, yellow pencil,
crossword puzzle from yesterday's paper,
her purse, the earrings someone removed,
polish on fingernails shining fresh.
She always had something to say.

We stay awake and wait for her return,
for blackberries to cover the fence,
her childhood farm in Ashland, Ohio,
the brick ranch in Hutchinson, Kansas
where holiday dinners flow year by year.

We wait for drifting snow,
the turn of season, turn of phrase,
the scent of steaming words, her pink face.

VACANT LOT

Old man gathers wood,
searches debris on bare ground,
tents zipped and dark, rolled blankets,
Trader Joe shopping cart, broken bike,
garbage stuffed in plastic bags.
They leave the sticks for me.

Every night more survivors,
the press of each arrival, each birth
pulling my death closer.
My body feels stretched and pegged,
gray pelt drying on a rack,
thin skin oozing blood like fog,
mist hugging the ground.

I remember lawn and trees
before the diesel demolition
left rotting beams and sheetrock
piled on living soil, suffocating all
with lime and gypsum,
the mound blocking sunlight,
my place to sleep.

Bones draped with loose skin,
dried sprigs of oak and cedar,
weak flame of morning fire,
the night with cooling ashes.

BUREAUCRACY ON THE BEACH

Pebbles stare like eyes in a bowl,
shells that once held living flesh
washed clean by the Committee to Pray for Rain.

They gather at the mossy river mouth
where sand flies dance on the edge of waves.

A wounded seal lies in backwash,
no umbrella to break the sun's current
hot as glass licked dry by tide and reef,
skin bursting like a grape.

Gulls swoop with crabs in their beaks
past blue plastic pebbles lining the sand
like stitches dropped by the Committee
to Ask Forgiveness. They meet over lunch
along the smudgy horizon.

The seal watches them with cloudy eyes,
its body buoyed in plasma surf
while fists of wood catch in a failed net
and blue-white waves chase tiny crabs
the shape of glass grapes.

The Committee for Plasma calls for stitches
much too late, their plastic veins the wrong color.

As if embarrassed for lying too long
the seal sinks deeper, guilt falling
in tides of sand. Seagulls watch

and return to claim the body, form
the Committee to Bury the Seal.

MAYBE THE SUN

Blame the stained curtains,
dingy rays on tablecloth,

my perma-press shirt yellowed
like old dentures. Or the Verona
coffee beans slick with roasting oil

ground a second too long,
their brew corrupt and bitter.

Mealy clumps of flour, pancakes
thin and rigid like eyelids straining
to open, pinned by syrupy threads.

Weeping fog, sappy redwood drools
pooling in ice between roots.

Frost on leaning granite.
The news last night,
the late party next door,

garbage trucks beeping backup,
cracking dead branches.

I should have gotten up
to shutter out the neighborhood.
Switched off the sun.

PEELING THE HANDLE

My father's jackknife
shaves spears of sunlight
from a cloudless sky
as he chips scabs of red enamel
from the wooden handle,
white primer underneath, fresh skin.
My small hands ape his fingers.

He sits below me
on the steps to our door
slathered with battleship gray,
my mother in the kitchen
boiling potatoes.

In a later year
they show me a dull gray photo,
thick boards of the stoop firmly nailed,
the Quonset hut with lace curtains,
door set in its corrugated curve,
bare yard, pale 1950 Chevrolet.

When I recall that morning
on the steps, my mother laughs,
another infant invention.
But I know she worried,
the potatoes boiling over
those nights he came home late,

stories she thought I would not remember,
how she waited for three years,
how they eloped after the war,
hope chest stuffed with lace and sterile gauze,
the veteran housing on an old base
ten miles of gravel from his new job,
farther in the drifting snow.

I never learned why
she asked him to whittle the handle
though the masher looked so odd
with patches of red and white.
Was it the grip or the peeling paint,
gritty flakes when she chewed?
Or was it the pinewood steps,
the temporary apartment far from home?
Or the one thing she could control.

FOOTSTEPS

The floor remembers your footsteps
I hear them when I try to clean
their echo evading my broom and mop
their ridges like zeroes carved in slate
but how can something denote nothing

like the woody bract of a pinecone
after the seeds have dropped
I imagine pine nuts everywhere
some I frame like photographs
others fall into my hair
kiss the leaves of my daily salad

even on days when I swear not to eat
they mark a trail toward the trees
if only I could follow

ROSE BOY

My mother blamed the surgeon
who cut out the red birthmark
bulging on my toddler arm,
but it sprouted instead,
leaves unfolding like tiny hands
until the vine extended past my wrist,
thorns scratching tattoo scars.

Each year more branches.
Walking down Mill Street
swaying like a stretched umbrella,
neighbors duck as I pass.
Some pause on warmer days,
grateful for my shade
and the clinging scent of blossoms,
but they avoid my embrace.

This is the life I live.
Service door, back row,
gnarled toes clutching carpet,
my fingers picking thorns like scabs,
exposing veins, bleeding sap,
shunned. Neither bush nor man.

One more spring is all I ask,
a homely bed of soil
to lay my drying hips,

an understanding voice,
one more slice of loving knife.

LETTER FROM HOME

You stopped being the person he knew
and became a pickup truck with bad springs.

The spaces you left
fill the rusted bed, suck you backward,
grind like loose teeth when you accelerate,
reset your iPhone, username, passwords.

Maybe you no longer feel surrounded,
whoever you are now. You left
before the posse converged,
too few to make a difference anyway,
your list of conditions he never understood,
and his as well.

He will never admit
he circles his own highway
searching for you, the scent of your exhaust,
the way your voice rises on tiptoes,
the twist of your chin and shoulder
when you make a point, punching air.

He speaks in past tense,
broken vase, shovel gouge in sheetrock,
your room untouched
as if you were already dead
the ghostly pain of his silent plea.

I DIED TO WRITE THIS POEM

There was no pain, only longing,
the way the canopy of stars replaces sky,
mourners wondering who will get my chair,
the cake with my misspelled name,
my last breath stumbling on goodbye
like a guest who stayed too long
trying to hide my coffee puddle
as if I dumped it on purpose
too close to my calculator,
the slide rule that became a joke,
mechanical pencils no one else can use,
drawing paper and ammonia-scented prints.

I was the engineer without a degree
who arrived from somewhere east,
secret agent from the land of words
where algorithms fall like slushy snow,
stick to my fingers in icy lines of code,
where I learned to test each step
like a farmer crossing a frozen pond
watching for bubbles, the fearful crack,
the flash of sun and early thaw,
reflections of a man they hardly knew,

but I was submerged already,
barely breathing, left for dead,
waiting to kick the bottom and rise,
the new moon hanging like a quill.

FEAR OF SPRING

You finish the project and then you wait
as if it were a seed pressed in damp soil
with whatever moisture you have left.

For days you stare at the surface, knowing
you can't turn back, no longer possible,
nor can you savor victory, less than it should be.

You could have done more. Maybe it's not too late,
one more shake of fertilizer but that would risk
burning the seed in its compost womb, the web

of old roots, leaves, stalks that once stood tall
now dead and moldering. The moment squeezes
shell and germ--outside your skin, inside your veins.

You watch yourself approach, that way
you fake your swagger, afraid to arrive.

RUMOR OF LOVE

Tonight we hide behind pseudonyms
trying to guess our subtext like literature freshmen:
should I prune my hair, will it grow more shoots?

That Christmas we found a bird's nest in the tree,
an omen for our lives in this former pasture,

how I wrote the philosophy essay for our son,
his only C, the handful of nails I left on the deck,

my lost keys, the rusty bucket of rainwater
bursting with mosquito larvae, the hint of malice
in my runny nose, how you always carry tissue

even when I'm swinging upside down,
never forget the secret cadence of my name.

Those first moments of our breathless romance
swept into the slip stream of a sixteen-wheeler
blowing out these walls so we could dance.

Did I ever tell you I lost my keys on purpose,
that age does not exist, that our discarded gestures
live on like a rumor no one else will ever share?

AGAIN THE SUPERMOON

Nights when the moon is close
tides of blood rush through my body,
draw me toward the shore of clouds
as you try to pull me back.

I hear the buoy in my ears,
the bells that think they know me,
have seen me before,
the same cliff, same alarm.

I should know its direction
but I am lost

craving the first snow,
the humidity colder than frost,
the silent time alone.

Leave the door open for me.

CORRECTION

I said I was sorry
to make you go away.

One more apology was all it took
like a gutter weighed down with wet pine straw
pulling nails from the eaves.

Outside my window the Monterey pine
throws more needles, tiny spears bending in wind,
thatching the asphalt roof, seeping rain.

Soaring to the highest limb, a solitary crow
clutches the season's last plum in its beak.

For once I caw back,
weary of plums, their tart skin.

ROBOT WRITES A LOVE POEM

Cabinets of shimmering glass,
halogen bulbs arrayed like sheep
in cliffy canyons, fallow suns
piercing loud scattered sky.

Your stainless contacts open,
fingers of reaching lilies
glinting gold, connected.

My memory is yours,
how you stoke my algorithms,
no blank lines between us.

Every word recalls another,
meta code compiled just for this,
the dry kiss of interface,
static grounding through our frames.

Routines we spawn,
screens filled with airy blips,
floating decimals like sleep.

Fans of warm breath
cool our heatsinks, motherboards
humming together, fading,
zero to one to zero.

INTERVIEW FOR A JOB AS POET

The HR intern asks me to compose a poem
and recite it extemporaneously,
but that's not how I write: I can't
call a poem to my lap like an Australian poodle,
no, I don't mean *Australian*, I mean *spaniel*
drooling and submissive, hoping to be caught,
but not a spaniel either, say *Spanish* like the flu,
germy similes with cilia massaging my tongue,
the tingle from my mother's baby aspirin,
an itchy virus sneaking up my back sinuses
until I sneeze tendrils into the water glass,
floating like pale roots from a cutting of English ivy
the same plant she grew on her brick wall
somewhere south of Minneapolis
only the south side she cautioned,
leave the north to the Irish, left-handed like me,
why I think I can write she always says,
that or too many dents in the cans of beer
I discarded on purpose when I worked at Safeway,
poems that made her shake her head so hard
they foamed when she popped them open
flat like a prescription, but not the same ivy,
call it the son of the son of the ivy, or daughter
yes daughter with pointy green hair,
the girl she always wanted, dressed me
in softball bloomers with ribbon cuffs,
a photo from another century

as if they knew the secret of aspirin
before the Spanish Flu, discovered
the obscurity of words like genes and gender,
dogs that look like cats, cough hairballs
into their beer, laugh through their noses,
a retriever scratching the germs in its ear,
how it can detect the discordant smell
of illness, of a poet needing a paycheck
choking on interview phlegm
as he tries to swallow another failure
like the day the manager at Safeway
asked me about the beer cans.

ABOUT THE AUTHOR

Terry Tierney is the author of a poetry collection, *The Poet's Garage*, and the novels *Lucky Ride* and *The Bridge on Beer River*, all published by *Unsolicited Press*. His poems, short stories, and reviews have appeared in numerous literary magazines. After serving in the Seabees, he completed his BA and MA at Binghamton University and a PhD in Victorian Literature at Emory University. He taught college composition and creative writing courses, and survived several Silicon Valley startups as a software engineering manager. He lives in the San Francisco Bay Area with his wife and literary mentor, Michaelyn Burnette, their enthusiastic Golden Retriever, and two fluffy cats. More can be learned at http://terrytierney.com

ABOUT THE PRESS

Unsolicited Press is based out of Portland, Oregon and focuses on the works of the unsung and underrepresented. As a womxn-owned, all-volunteer small publisher that doesn't worry about profits as much as championing exceptional literature, we have the privilege of partnering with authors skirting the fringes of the lit world. We've worked with emerging and award-winning authors such as Shann Ray, Amy Shimshon-Santo, Brook Bhagat, Kris Amos, and John W. Bateman.

Learn more at unsolicitedpress.com. Find us on twitter and instagram.